HOW DOES SANTA ALL THOSE GIFTS ON CHRISTMAS EVE?

How does Santa deliver all those gifts on Christmas Eve?

Text copyright © 2023 by Michael Zema

Illustrations copyright © Canva.com

Illustrations copyright © Riley Leider

All rights reserved. No part of this publication may be reproduced or used in any manner without the prior written permission of the copyright owner, except for the use of brief quotations in a book review.

ISBN: 9798867033316

Copyright Registration No.: TXu 2-327-665

I would like to dedicate this book to my wife, children and grandchildren.

Thank you to: Riley Leider, Ann Leider and Lynzee Wig for helping to make this book possible.

For years, Santa and the Elves have spent days and nights making toys for girls and boys that would be delivered all over the world.

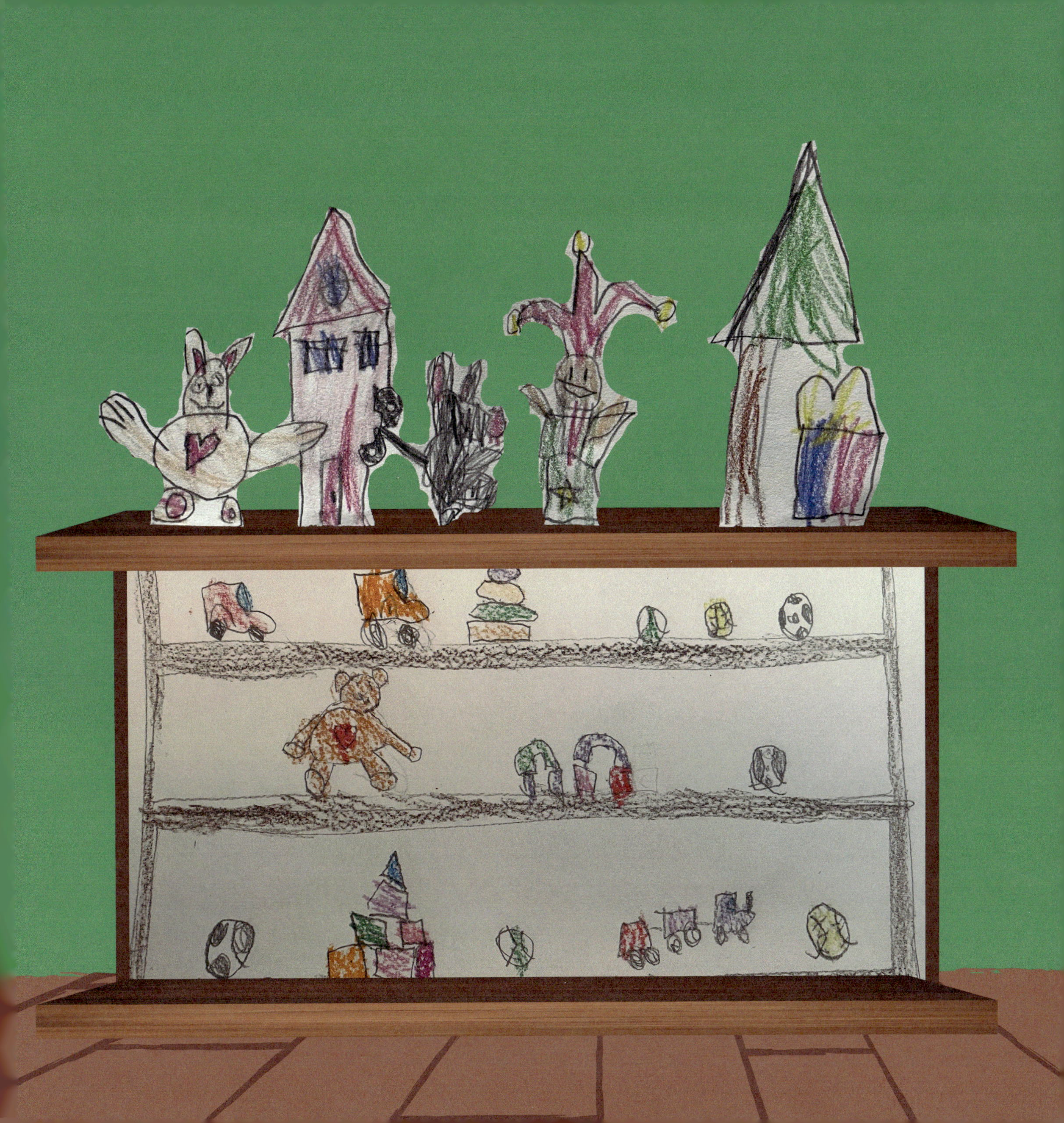

Mrs. Claus would carefully check each child's name from Santa's list, then on Christmas Eve. Santa, Mrs. Claus, and the Elves would load up the sled, for their long journey to deliver all the gifts.

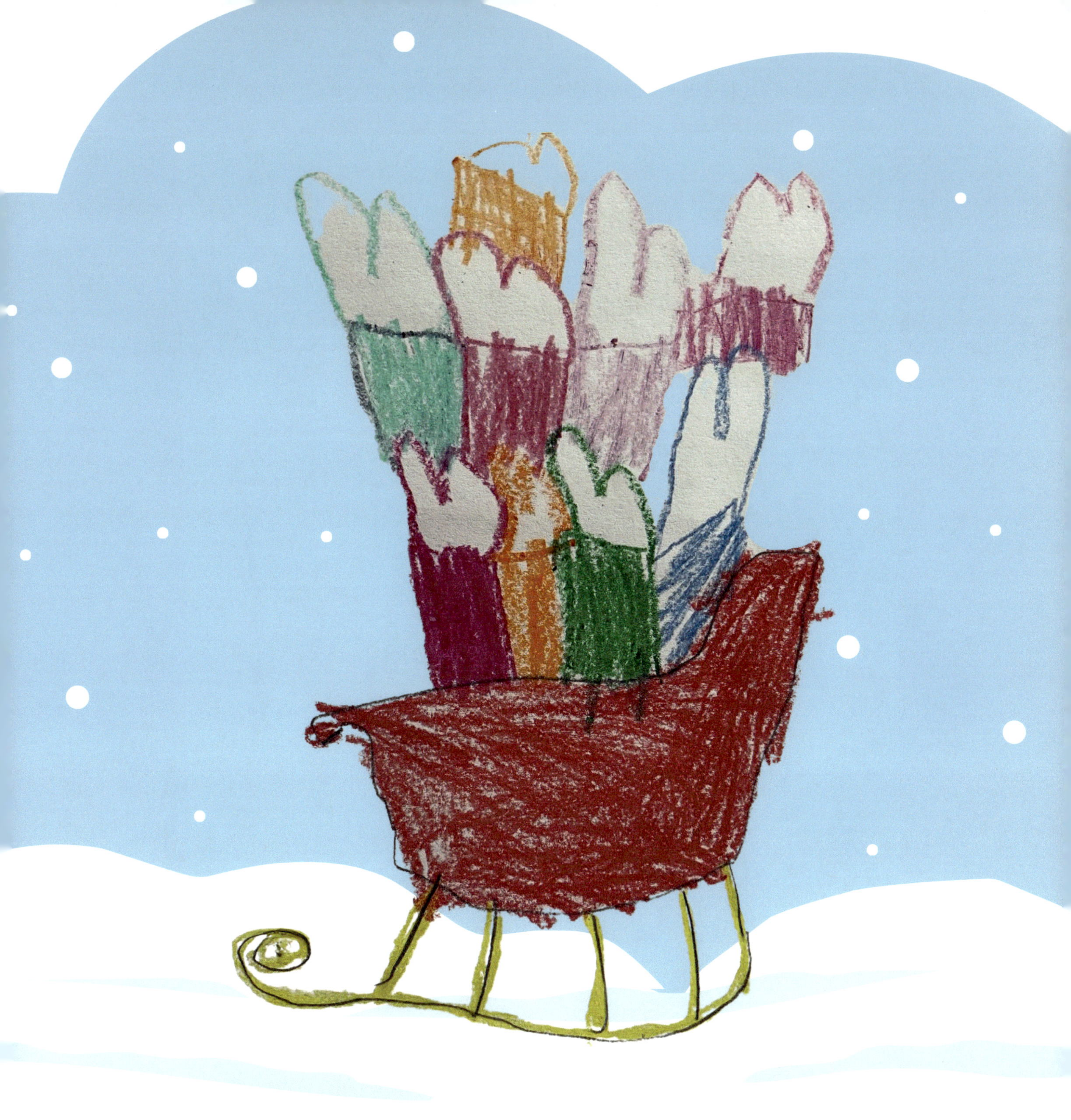

Now Santa never gave much thought in how he was able to deliver all those gifts.

He knew it was just Christmas Magic and did not give much thought about it.

And this is where the story begins.

Christopher was like many little boys and girls and was getting excited for Christmas to arrive, so Christopher decided it was time to sit down and begin writing his Christmas list.

Since he was old enough to write, he always tried to complete his list weeks in advance of Christmas so his mother or father could mail his letter to the North Pole.

Now Christopher was not a greedy boy, and only had a few items on his list. He always included a final wish for peace and happiness throughout the world.

Peace and Happiness

While Christopher was writing this list, a thought came to him.

He had become curious as to how Santa could deliver all those gifts to children all over the world in one night, so he decided to include this question in his letter.

Now Christopher's little brother Liam thought he had the answer and told Christopher that he thinks Santa put a jet engine on his sled. Christopher told Liam he didn't think Santa would do this.

A few weeks later Christopher was shopping with his parents at the mall when he saw Santa sitting on his chair with lots of children waiting patiently to see him.

Christopher was so excited and pleaded with his parents to see and talk with Santa.

Christopher's parents knew Santa was at the mall and wanted to surprise him with the visit.

When it was his turn to see Santa, he told Santa that he had been a good boy helping with the chaos at home, respected his family and friends, and was very excited about Christmas.

Christopher thought as long as Santa was here he would ask the question, "How can you deliver all the gifts that children asked for all over the world in one evening?"

Not expecting this question Santa replied, "Christmas Magic my boy."

Believe in the magic of Christmas!

When Santa went back to the North Pole, he noticed that more and more of the letters from boys and girls included this question about how he delivers all the gifts in one night.

While having dinner with Mrs. Claus he shared with her the question so many children started to ask, "How can Santa deliver all these gifts in one night?"

Mrs. Claus said she also noticed more of the children were asking this question in their letters. Her advice was to share with the children how he does it.

In responding to the children's letters, he decided to share with them that the magic was about time.
He gave the example to the children of when they fall asleep and begin to dream, their dreams seem to only last for a few minutes. But, they have slept through the night.

On Christmas Eve Santa actually stops time just like in a dream and the only people moving about are Santa, reindeer and his helpers.

What most children didn't know is that throughout the year Santa calls some grandmas and grandpas to help him. On Christmas Eve he gives them magical powers
to help him deliver gifts
to boys and girls all over the world.

GAMMY

PAPA

So now boys and girls when someone ask you how Santa Claus can deliver all those gifts you can share with them the story of how he does it.

Do you think your grandma and grandpa are some of Santa's Helpers?

¡Feliz Navidad!

圣诞节快乐!
(Shèngdàn jié kuàilè!)

Hyvää Joulua!

Buon Natale!

Joyeux Noël!

Feliz Natal!

God Jul!

Wesołych Świąt!

Merry Christmas Everyone!

Nollaig Shona!

Frohe Weihnachten!

Made in the USA
Columbia, SC
29 November 2024